What I love about you, Mom

What I love about you, Mom

Kate Marshall & David Marshall

A PLUME BOOK

PLUME
Published by Penguin Group
Penguin Group (USA) Inc., 375 Hudson Street, New York, New York 10014, USA
Penguin Group (Canada), 90 Eglinton Avenue East, Suite 700, Toronto, Ontario M4P 2Y3, Canada
    (a division of Pearson Penguin Canada Inc.)
Penguin Books Ltd, 80 Strand, London WC2R 0RL, England
Penguin Ireland, 25 St Stephen's Green, Dublin 2, Ireland (a division of Penguin Books Ltd)
Penguin Group (Australia), 707 Collins Street, Melbourne, Victoria 3008, Australia
    (a division of Pearson Australia Group Pty Ltd)
Penguin Books India Pvt Ltd, 11 Community Centre, Panchsheel Park, New Delhi – 110 017, India
Penguin Group (NZ), 67 Apollo Drive, Rosedale, Auckland 0632, New Zealand (a division of Pearson New Zealand Ltd)
Penguin Books, Rosebank Office Park, 181 Jan Smuts Avenue, Parktown North 2193, South Africa
Penguin China, B7 Jiaming Center, 27 East Third Ring Road North, Chaoyang District, Beijing 100020, China

First published by Plume, a member of Penguin Group (USA) Inc.

First Printing, April 2013
10 9 8 7 6 5 4 3 2 1

Ⓟ REGISTERED TRADEMARK—MARCA REGISTRADA

ISBN 978-0-452-29847-7

BOOK DESIGN: Catherine Leonardo

ALWAYS LEARNING   PEARSON

What I love about you, Mom

Date: _____

For (full name):

_____

From (full name):

_____

Dear Mom,

I've enlisted the help of this journal to tell you how wonderful you are and to thank you for all you've done for me. If I've forgotten to write, checkmark, or draw anything in these pages, it's because *I'm* imperfect, not you. Thank you for everything.

Love,

_____

Early Days

Here's a picture of us when I was young . . .

(Add a photo, sketch, or doodle)

Early Days

One of my earliest memories of you is . . .

_____

_____

_____

_____

_____

When I close my eyes and picture a typical
day at home when I was a child, you are . . .

(Where, doing what, wearing what, with whom . . .)

_____

_____

_____

_____

_____

_____

_____

_____

Sounds and smells I associate
with you from my childhood . . .

*(Oldies music, your laugh, jingling keys, sizzling bacon,
sunscreen, fresh laundry, perfume, other)*

_____

_____

_____

_____

I love this funny family story
about the time you . . .

_____

_____

_____

_____

_____

_____

Early Days

I used to love it when you . . .

_____

_____

_____

_____

_____

_____

_____

You were a hero to me when . . .

_____

_____

_____

_____

_____

_____

_____

_____

Early Days

My memory may be fuzzy about some of my "firsts," but it means a lot to me that you were there for so many of these milestones:

(Check all that apply)

☐ Starting preschool

☐ Starting kindergarten

☐ Learning to read

☐ My first sleepover with friend(s)

☐ Learning to ride a bike

☐ Learning to swim

☐ First airplane flight

☐ Learning to drive

☐ When I got my first pet _____ _____

☐ The loss of _____ _____

☐ Joining _____ _____

☐ Doing a science fair or project

☐ School play or concert

☐ Starting middle/junior high school

☐ Starting high school

☐ First job _____ _____

☐ First date

☐ First prom/formal dance

☐ Award/achievement _____ _____ _____

☐ Voting for the first time

☐ Graduating from high school

☐ Leaving home for _____ _____

☐ Graduating from _____ _____

☐ Other _____ _____

Early Days

Even if I didn't always open up, I appreciate
that you were also there for me when I:

(Check all that apply)

☐ was sick _____

☐ hurt myself _____

☐ had important decisions to make

☐ had trouble with siblings or friends

☐ was in a bad mood

☐ rebelled or tested limits

_____

_____

_____

_____

_____

_____

_____

_____

_____

_____

_____

Early Days

When I was young, you were most like this beloved fictional mom:

☐ Marmee March (*Little Women*)

☐ Caroline Ingalls (*Little House on the Prairie*)

☐ Horton (*Horton Hatches the Egg*)

☐ Mother bunny (*The Runaway Bunny*)

☐ Lucille Ricardo (*I Love Lucy*)

☐ Donna Reed (*The Donna Reed Show*)

☐ Wilma Flintstone (*The Flintstones*)

☐ Laura Petrie (*The Dick Van Dyke Show*)

☐ Mama Bear (*Berenstain Bears*)

☐ Maria von Trapp (*The Sound of Music*)

☐ Claire Huxtable (*The Cosby Show*)

☐ Marge Simpson (*The Simpsons*)

☐ Mrs. Gump (*Forrest Gump*)

☐ Debra Barone (*Everybody Loves Raymond*)

☐ Molly Weasley (*Harry Potter*)

☐ Lorelai Gilmore (*Gilmore Girls*)

☐ Claire Dunphy (*Modern Family*)

☐ Other _____

_____

_____

I am sorry that when I was young . . .

_____
_____
_____
_____
_____
_____
_____

Now that I'm a parent myself,
I have a whole new appreciation for . . .

_____
_____
_____
_____
_____
_____
_____

Early Days

More childhood memories of you and me . . .

*(Bedtime rituals, games we played, books we read, presents,
holidays, stories, photos, or drawings . . .)*

Early Days

Childhood memories . . .

Early Days

Childhood memories . . .

Admiring You

You are:

(Circle or add the five or six most fitting describing words)

affectionate	happy	smart
brave	honest	spiritual
calm	imaginative	spontaneous
careful	introspective	steady
caring	loving	stoic
confident	optimistic	strong
considerate	passionate	stylish
creative	patient	supportive
curious	patriotic	sweet
determined	persistent	thrifty
disciplined	persuasive	tolerant
dramatic	philosophical	tough
energetic	playful	wise
flexible	practical	_____
friendly	protective	_____
funny	responsible	_____
generous	self-reliant	_____
gentle	sensitive	_____

Admiring You

One word that captures *you* is . . .

(Pick one describing word and use the full page to write it in LARGE, decorative letters or to illustrate the word)

Admiring You

You are strong or unique in this way . . .

_____

_____

_____

_____

_____

_____

_____

You are really good at . . .

_____

_____

_____

_____

_____

_____

_____

Admiring You

You seem happy when . . .

_____

_____

_____

_____

_____

_____

_____

My favorite food that you make is . . .

_____

_____

_____

_____

_____

_____

_____

_____

Admiring You

The President should award you the highest honor for this past or present achievement:

*(Pancake making, joke telling, bargain hunting,
work and family balancing, Easter egg hiding, other)*

_____ (name)

is hereby awarded the title of

_____ in recognition

of her exemplary service and talent in

the field of _____

Admiring You

I hope I've inherited half your . . .

(Sense of humor, good nature, smarts, toughness, good looks, other)

_____

_____

_____

_____

_____

_____

I see bits of your likeness or personality
in these other family members . . .

_____

_____

_____

_____

_____

_____

Roses are red,
Violets are blue,

_____

_____

Admiring You

This song, book, show or movie
makes me think of you . . .

_____

_____

_____

_____

_____

_____

If I had a quarter for every
time you said this, I'd be rich . . .

_____

_____

_____

_____

_____

_____

Admiring You

When you are in the room, everything is:

(Circle the best one or two)

livelier

warmer

calmer

safer

funnier

smarter

prettier

complete

_____

_____

_____

_____

Admiring You

If you were a book, you'd be:

☐ a mystery (full of surprises)

☐ a romance (all about love, love, love)

☐ a fairy tale (virtuous, prevailing)

☐ a poem (efficient, thoughtful)

☐ a Western (strong, pioneering)

☐ nonfiction (practical, instructive)

☐ a comedy (witty, fun)

☐ a fantasy (magical, fanciful)

☐ science fiction (full of bold ideas)

☐ a memoir (such an interesting life)

_____

_____

_____

_____

_____

Admiring You

If you write your autobiography—
and I hope you do—you should call it . . .

_____

_____

This could be the book cover
or movie poster for your life story . . .

(Design a book cover or movie poster)

Admiring You

I associate these flowers or plants with you:

(Circle or add flower, plant, tree, vegetable, herb)

Carnations	Orchids	Apple tree
Daffodils	Pansies	Maple tree
Daisies	Roses	Basil
Geraniums	Thistles	Tomato plant
Lavender	Tulips	_____
Lilies	Violets	_____

And here's why:

_____

_____

_____

_____

_____

Admiring You

These are the colors I think of for you:

(Circle or add colors)

Pink	Light blue	Gray
Maroon	Turquoise	White
Red	Violet	Beige
Orange	Lavender	Tan
Yellow	Purple	Brown
Light green	Gold	_____
Dark green	Silver	_____
Dark blue	Black	_____

And here's why:

_____

_____

_____

_____

Admiring You

This is the name your grandchildren call you
(or what I imagine they will) and why . . .

_____

_____

_____

_____

_____

_____

This was one of my favorite moments watching
you with a grandchild (or what I predict will be) . . .

_____

_____

_____

_____

_____

_____

Admiring You

This is a wonderful gift, tradition, or lesson that you passed on to your grandchildren (or that I hope you will) . . .

_____

_____

_____

_____

One of the best parenting tips
you gave or modeled was . . .

_____

_____

_____

_____

I know your grandchildren will
remember this about you . . .

_____

_____

_____

_____

Admiring You

You are . . .

Admiring You

You are . . .

Appreciating You

I'm filling this box with hugs for you
to use anytime you need them:

(Fill the whole box using color or your favorite pattern)

sample patterns

Appreciating You

I know I wasn't much of a talker before
I turned two, so I'd like to thank you now for:

(Check or star all that apply)

____ Sleepless nights up with me

____ Holding me while I cried

____ Changing my diapers

____ Wiping mashed food off my face

____ Buttoning, zipping, lacing me up

____ Taking me to the doctor

____ Keeping me safe from harm

____ Scaring away the monsters

____ Countless bedtime stories

____ Entertaining me

____ Worrying about me

____ Introducing me to the world

Appreciating You

Come to think of it, I might not
have taken the time to thank you when
I was a bit older either. Thank you for:

(Check or star all that apply)

_____ Helping with homework

_____ Going to Back-to-School Nights

_____ Packing endless lunches

_____ Driving me all over

_____ Hosting my playdates

_____ Making birthdays special

_____ Coming to my games or shows

_____ Shopping with or for me

_____ Keeping the refrigerated stocked

_____ Making me eat vegetables

Appreciating You

You probably saw I enjoyed it, but
did I actually *thank* you back then
for taking me to these places?:

(Circle outings enjoyed)

Restaurants or picnics

Movies or shows

The library or book store

Shopping

The park

Fairs or amusement parks

Nature walks

Bike rides

Swimming

Camp

Museums or the zoo

Vacations

_____

_____

Appreciating You

I also want to thank you, Mom, for:

(Okay to adapt, for example,
"Helping ~~me~~ grandpa when he was sick")

Helping me _____

_____

_____

Pushing me to _____

_____

_____

Making sure that I _____

_____

_____

Letting me _____

_____

_____

Encouraging me to _____

_____

_____

Appreciating You

Putting up with me when _____

_____

_____

Coming to the rescue when _____

_____

_____

Making me feel _____

_____

_____

Introducing me to _____

_____

_____

Supporting my decision to _____

_____

_____

Helping me get through _____

_____

_____

Appreciating You

I'm thankful that you brought me up to try to be:

(Circle the four or five best words)

adventurous	health conscious
ambitious	independent
assertive	inquisitive
brave	kind
careful	loyal
caring	musical
conservative	nature-loving
creative	optimistic
cultured	progressive
curious	spiritual
ethical	stylish
faithful	well-mannered
family-oriented	_____
frugal	_____
hardworking	_____
	_____

Appreciating You

It meant a lot to me when you . . .

*(Cheered, accepted, advised, gave,
stood up for, visited, comforted, other)*

_____

_____

_____

_____

_____

_____

I was or am happy that you are my mother when . . .

_____

_____

_____

_____

_____

_____

_____

Appreciating You

I have especially appreciated your help or talents in:

(Check three or four favorites from this list)

☐ animal care

☐ arts & crafts

☐ baking & cooking

☐ cleaning & organizing

☐ entertaining

☐ fixing things

☐ gardening

☐ health & fitness

☐ home decorating

☐ home remedies

☐ making friends

☐ making music

☐ making people laugh

☐ math & science

☐ money matters

☐ raising children

☐ relationships

☐ spirituality

☐ telling jokes

☐ telling stories

☐ traveling

☐ work/career

☐ writing

_____

_____

_____

_____

_____

Don't be surprised if I call you for advice about . . .

_____

_____

_____

_____

_____

_____

Of the many gifts you've given me
over the years, this one stands out . . .

_____

_____

_____

_____

_____

_____

Appreciating You

My acceptance speech for my Olympic medal,
Nobel Prize, Pulitzer Prize, Academy, Emmy, or Grammy
Award *(circle which)* for _____
will conclude with . . .

_____

_____

_____

_____

_____

_____

". . . and last but not least, I want to thank my mother, for

_____

_____

_____

_____

_____

_____

_____

_____

_____" (queue music)

Okay, I admit it. You were right, I should . . .

(Do this, go there, stop this, start that . . . or should have)

_____

_____

_____

_____

I haven't always been the perfect child.
I'm sorry that . . .

(Words, deed, absence, bother, mistake, other)

_____

_____

_____

Thank you for *not* . . .

(Doing, saying, hinting, being . . .)

_____

_____

_____

Appreciating You

Just as young children often make handprint art
as a gift for their mothers, I offer you here
an outline of my hand *now* . . .

(Outline hand with pen and decorate [optional])

Appreciating You

You might think I haven't been listening, but I have. Here are some life lessons I've learned from you:

(Don't grocery shop while hungry, tip well, choose friends wisely, never stop learning)

Top 5 List—Mom's Life Lessons

1. _____

2. _____

3. _____

4. _____

5. _____

Appreciating You

Through your thoughts, words, and deeds
in the community, at work, and elsewhere,
you have touched many lives, including:

(Label the shapes with names of people, animals, causes, or organizations)

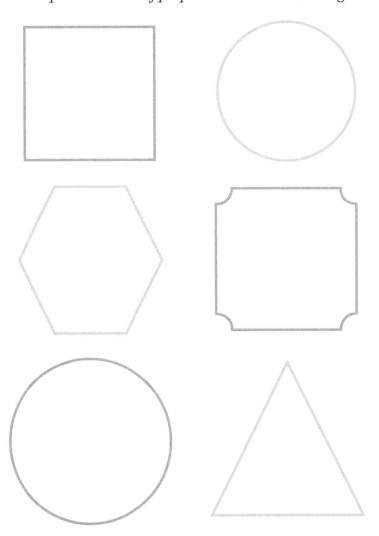

Appreciating You

In short, thank you, Mom, for:

1. _____

_____

2. _____

_____

3. _____

_____

Appreciating You

Just in case I haven't said it enough,
I'm filling this page by writing "thank you"
as many times or in as many ways as I can . . .

(Cover page with thank-yous using different lettering, styles, or languages)

Appreciating You

Thank you . . .

Thank you . . .

Enjoying Us

This makes me smile . . .

(Add photo, drawing, or memento)

Enjoying Us

WHEN I WAS YOUNG, YOU WERE MOSTLY MY:	NOW YOU ARE MOSTLY MY:
_____ manager	_____ manager
_____ teacher	_____ teacher
_____ coach	_____ coach
_____ counselor	_____ counselor
_____ mentor	_____ mentor
_____ friend	_____ friend
_____	_____

Enjoying Us

What a time we had together recently when . . .

(Fun, touching, exciting, surprising, other time)

_____

_____

_____

_____

_____

_____

Here's something I wish we could
do together more often . . .

_____

_____

_____

_____

_____

_____

_____

Enjoying Us

One of my favorite rituals or traditions
to share with you is . . .

(Holiday meal, birthday phone call, other)

_____

_____

_____

_____

_____

_____

_____

I love hearing you tell this story or talk about . . .

_____

_____

_____

_____

_____

_____

_____

_____

Enjoying Us

Here's a gift certificate for you:

(Hug, chore, treat, outing, phone call, letter, visit, other)

Gift Certificate

This certificate is good for:

_____

_____

_____

_____

_____

Enjoying Us

I'm really looking forward to having you in my life as I:

(Check or star what applies)

____ Graduate from school

____ Find and keep love

____ Get married

____ Take care of a home

____ Nurture my own children

____ Keep growing at work

____ Have adventures to share

____ Set and work toward my goals

____ Celebrate milestones and successes

____ Navigate transitions and challenges

_____

_____

_____

Enjoying Us

Two things I especially look forward to in our future:

1. _____

   _____

   _____

2. _____

   _____

   _____

Enjoying Us

Time together . . .

Enjoying Us

Time together . . .

My Wishes for You

If I could arrange for you to spend an
afternoon with *anyone* in the world—past,
present, or future—it would be . . .

_____

_____

_____

_____

_____

_____

_____

If I could take you *anywhere* in
the world, I'd take you to . . .

_____

_____

_____

_____

_____

_____

_____

My Wishes for You

If I could make three amazing things happen
for you by waving a magic wand, I'd . . .

1. _____

_____

_____

2. _____

_____

_____

3. _____

_____

_____

My promise to you:

_____

_____

_____

_____

_____

_____

_____

Lastly, the main thing I want to say to you is . . .

_____

_____

_____

_____

_____

_____

_____

Extra Pages

Messages from Others

*(Son-in-law, daughter-in-law, husband,
other children, grandchildren, other)*

Photos

Drawings

Mementos

News Clippings

Extra Pages

Extra Pages

Extra Pages

Extra Pages

Extra Pages

Extra Pages

Extra Pages

Extra Pages

Extra Pages

*H*usband and wife team KATE AND DAVID MARSHALL have been writing partners for over twenty years, creating guided journals that celebrate family, relationships, and personal growth. Whether telling a spouse or parent the many ways he or she is appreciated; encouraging an elder to write his memoirs; or helping someone clarify his or her personal dreams for the future, their books help loved ones communicate in enjoyable, informative, and often profound ways.

The Marshalls would love to hear from you at:

www.marshallbooks.net
Kate and David Marshall
P.O. Box 6846
Moraga, California 94570-6846

We dedicate this book to our mothers,

To your mothers,

And to unsung mothers everywhere.

You are all heroes.

—Kate and David Marshall